OECD/G20 Base Erosion and Profit Shifting Project

Making Dispute Resolution More Effective – MAP Peer Review Report, Macau, China (Stage 2)

INCLUSIVE FRAMEWORK ON BEPS: ACTION 14

This document, as well as any data and map included herein, are without prejudice to the status of or sovereignty over any territory, to the delimitation of international frontiers and boundaries and to the name of any territory, city or area.

Please cite this publication as:
OECD (2022), *Making Dispute Resolution More Effective – MAP Peer Review Report, Macau, China (Stage 2): Inclusive Framework on BEPS: Action 14*, OECD/G20 Base Erosion and Profit Shifting Project, OECD Publishing, Paris, https://doi.org/10.1787/df263845-en.

ISBN 978-92-64-84702-6 (print)
ISBN 978-92-64-91228-1 (pdf)

OECD/G20 Base Erosion and Profit Shifting Project
ISSN 2313-2604 (print)
ISSN 2313-2612 (online)

Photo credits: Cover © ninog-Fotolia.com

Corrigenda to publications may be found on line at: www.oecd.org/about/publishing/corrigenda.htm.
© OECD 2022

The use of this work, whether digital or print, is governed by the Terms and Conditions to be found at https://www.oecd.org/termsandconditions.

Foreword

Digitalisation and globalisation have had a profound impact on economies and the lives of people around the world, and this impact has only accelerated in the 21st century. These changes have brought with them challenges to the rules for taxing international business income, which have prevailed for more than a hundred years and created opportunities for base erosion and profit shifting (BEPS), requiring bold moves by policy makers to restore confidence in the system and ensure that profits are taxed where economic activities take place and value is created.

In 2013, the OECD ramped up efforts to address these challenges in response to growing public and political concerns about tax avoidance by large multinationals. The OECD and G20 countries joined forces and developed an Action Plan to address BEPS in September 2013. The Action Plan identified 15 actions aimed at introducing coherence in the domestic rules that affect cross-border activities, reinforcing substance requirements in the existing international standards, and improving transparency as well as certainty.

After two years of work, measures in response to the 15 actions, including those published in an interim form in 2014, were consolidated into a comprehensive package and delivered to G20 Leaders in November 2015. The BEPS package represents the first substantial renovation of the international tax rules in almost a century. As the BEPS measures are implemented, it is expected that profits will be reported where the economic activities that generate them are carried out and where value is created. BEPS planning strategies that rely on outdated rules or on poorly co-ordinated domestic measures will be rendered ineffective.

OECD and G20 countries also agreed to continue to work together to ensure a consistent and co-ordinated implementation of the BEPS recommendations and to make the project more inclusive. As a result, they created the OECD/G20 Inclusive Framework on BEPS (Inclusive Framework), bringing all interested and committed countries and jurisdictions on an equal footing in the Committee on Fiscal Affairs and its subsidiary bodies. With over 140 members, the Inclusive Framework monitors and peer reviews the implementation of the minimum standards and is completing the work on standard setting to address BEPS issues. In addition to its members, other international organisations and regional tax bodies are involved in the work of the Inclusive Framework, which also consults business and the civil society on its different work streams.

Although implementation of the BEPS package is dramatically changing the international tax landscape and improving the fairness of tax systems, one of the key outstanding BEPS issues – to address the tax challenges arising from the digitalisation of the economy – remained unresolved. In a major step forward on 8 October 2021, over 135 Inclusive Framework members, representing more than 95% of global GDP, joined a two-pillar solution to reform the international taxation rules and ensure that multinational enterprises pay a fair share of tax wherever they operate and generate profits in today's digitalised and globalised world economy. The implementation of these new rules is envisaged by 2023.

This report was approved by the Inclusive Framework on 17 March 2022 and prepared for publication by the OECD Secretariat.

Table of contents

Abbreviations and acronyms 7

Executive summary 9

    References 10

Introduction 11

Part A. Preventing disputes 15

    [A.1] Include Article 25(3), first sentence, of the OECD Model Tax Convention in tax treaties 15
    [A.2] Provide roll-back of bilateral APAs in appropriate cases 16

    References 17

Part B. Availability and access to MAP 19

    [B.1] Include Article 25(1) of the OECD Model Tax Convention in tax treaties 19
    [B.2] Allow submission of MAP requests to the competent authority of either treaty partner, or,
          alternatively, introduce a bilateral consultation or notification process 21
    [B.3] Provide access to MAP in transfer pricing cases 23
    [B.4] Provide access to MAP in relation to the application of anti-abuse provisions 24
    [B.5] Provide access to MAP in cases of audit settlements 25
    [B.6] Provide access to MAP if required information is submitted 27
    [B.7] Include Article 25(3), second sentence, of the OECD Model Tax Convention in tax treaties ... 28
    [B.8] Publish clear and comprehensive MAP guidance 29
    [B.9] Make MAP guidance available and easily accessible and publish MAP profile 31
    [B.10] Clarify in MAP guidance that audit settlements do not preclude access to MAP 32

    References 34

Part C. Resolution of MAP cases 35

    [C.1] Include Article 25(2), first sentence, of the OECD Model Tax Convention in tax treaties 35
    [C.2] Seek to resolve MAP cases within a 24-month average timeframe 36
    [C.3] Provide adequate resources to the MAP function 37
    [C.4] Ensure staff in charge of MAP has the authority to resolve cases in accordance with the
          applicable tax treaty 38
    [C.5] Use appropriate performance indicators for the MAP function 39
    [C.6] Provide transparency with respect to the position on MAP arbitration 40

    References 41

Part D. **Implementation of MAP agreements** 43
    [D.1]   Implement all MAP agreements 43
    [D.2]   Implement all MAP agreements on a timely basis 44
    [D.3]   Include Article 25(2), second sentence, of the OECD Model Tax Convention in tax treaties or alternative provisions in Article 9(1) and Article 7(2) 45

    Reference 46

Summary 47

Annex A. **Tax treaty network of Macau, China** 49

Annex B. **MAP Statistics Reporting for the 2016, 2017, 2018, 2019 and 2020 Reporting Periods (1 January 2016 to 31 December 2020) for pre-2016 cases** 51

Annex C. **MAP Statistics Reporting for the 2016, 2017, 2018, 2019 and 2020 Reporting Periods (1 January 2016 to 31 December 2020) for post-2015 cases** 54

Glossary 57

Abbreviations and acronyms

APA	Advance Pricing Arrangement
BEPS	Base Erosion and Profit Shifting
FTA	Forum on Tax Administration
MAP	Mutual Agreement Procedure
OECD	Organisation for Economic Co-operation and Development

Executive summary

Macau, China has a small tax treaty network with six tax treaties. Macau, China has a newly established MAP programme and has no experience with resolving MAP cases as it has not yet been involved in any cases. The outcome of the stage 1 peer review process was that overall Macau, China met the majority of the elements of the Action 14 Minimum Standard. Where it has deficiencies, Macau, China has worked to address them, which has been monitored in stage 2 of the process. In this respect, Macau, China has solved almost all the identified deficiencies.

All of Macau, China's tax treaties contain a provision relating to MAP. Those treaties mostly follow paragraphs 1 through 3 of Article 25 of the OECD Model Tax Convention (OECD, 2017). Its treaty network is consistent with the requirements of the Action 14 Minimum Standard, except for the fact that:

- One out of Macau, China's six tax treaties does not contain the equivalent of Article 25(1), first sentence of the OECD Model Tax Convention (OECD, 2015a) as it read prior to the adoption of the Action 14 final report (OECD, 2015b) since it does not allow taxpayers to submit a MAP request to the state of which it is a national, where its case comes under the non-discrimination provision.

- One out of Macau, China's six tax treaties does not contain the equivalent of Article 25(3), second sentence of the OECD Model Tax Convention (OECD, 2017) stating that the competent authorities may consult together for the elimination of double taxation for cases not provided for in the tax treaty.

In order to be fully compliant with all four key areas of an effective dispute resolution mechanism under the Action 14 Minimum Standard, Macau, China needs to amend and update two tax treaties. Macau, China reported that it intends to update all of its tax treaties via bilateral negotiations to be compliant with the requirements under the Action 14 Minimum Standard, and has already started the negotiation with one of its treaty partners. Once this treaty negotiation has concluded, Macau, China will initiate negotiations with the remaining treaty partner.

As Macau, China has no bilateral APA programme in place, there were no further elements to assess regarding the prevention of disputes.

Macau, China meets almost all of the requirements regarding availability and access to MAP under the Action 14 Minimum Standard. It provides access to MAP in all eligible cases in principle, although it has since 1 September 2019 not received any MAP request concerning transfer pricing cases, cases where anti-abuse provisions are applied. Furthermore, Macau, China has in place a documented bilateral notification process for those situations in which its competent authority considers the objection raised by taxpayers in a MAP request as not justified. Finally, Macau, China has clear and comprehensive guidance on the availability of MAP and how it applies this procedure in practice.

Macau, China has not been involved in any MAP cases since 1 January 2016, but meets in principle all the requirements under the Action 14 Minimum Standard in relation to the resolution of MAP cases. Macau, China's competent authority operates fully independently from the audit function of the tax authorities and envisages a co-operative approach to resolve MAP cases in an effective and efficient manner. Its organisation is adequate and the performance indicators used are appropriate to evaluate the MAP function.

Lastly, Macau, China in principle meets the Action 14 Minimum Standard as regards the implementation of MAP agreements. Macau, China would monitor the implementation of such agreements.

References

OECD (2015a), *Model Tax Convention on Income and on Capital 2014 (Full Version)*, OECD Publishing, Paris, https://dx.doi.org/10.1787/9789264239081-en.

OECD (2015b), "Making Dispute Resolution Mechanisms More Effective, Action 14 – 2015 Final Report", in *OECD/G20 Base Erosion and Profit Shifting Project*, OECD Publishing, Paris, https://dx.doi.org/10.1787/9789264241633-en.

OECD (2017), *Model Tax Convention on Income and on Capital 2017 (Full Version)*, OECD Publishing, Paris, https://dx.doi.org/10.1787/g2g972ee-en.

Introduction

Available mechanisms in Macau, China to resolve tax treaty-related disputes

Macau, China has entered into six tax treaties on income (and/or capital), four of which are in force.[1] These six treaties are being applied to an equal number of jurisdictions. All of these treaties provide for a mutual agreement procedure ("**MAP**") for resolving disputes on the interpretation and application of the provisions of the tax treaty. None of these treaties include an arbitration procedure as a final stage to the mutual agreement procedure.

Under Macau, China's tax treaties, the competent authority function is assigned to the Chief Executive of Macau, China. In practice, this function has been delegated to Macau, China's Financial Services Bureau. The competent authority of Macau, China currently employs four staff members, who would be responsible for both attribution/allocation and other MAP cases in addition to other tax treaty related tasks.

Macau, China has issued guidance on the governance and administration of the MAP which was last updated in June 2021, and is available (in English) at:

www.dsf.gov.mo/download/tax/E_MAPGuidelines.pdf

Developments in Macau, China since 1 September 2019

Developments in relation to the tax treaty network

The stage 1 report noted that Macau, China was conducting tax treaty negotiations with Cambodia and negotiating an amending protocol to the treaty with Mozambique. Macau, China reported that this situation remains the same with respect to Mozambique whereas a new treaty has been signed with Cambodia as noted below. The stage 1 report also noted that Macau, China had signed a treaty with Belgium, which had not yet entered into force. This situation remains the same.

In addition, Macau, China reported that it has signed a new tax treaty with Cambodia (2021) which is a newly negotiated treaty with a treaty partner with which there was no treaty yet in place. This treaty includes Article 9(2) and Article 25(1-3) of the OECD Model Tax Convention (OECD, 2017). This treaty has not yet entered into force.

For the two treaties that are considered not to be in line with one or more elements of the Action 14 Minimum Standard, Macau, China reported that it intends to update them via bilateral negotiations. In this respect, Macau, China reported that it has initiated negotiations with one treaty partner and that once these negotiations are concluded, it would initiate negotiations with the remaining treaty partner.

Other developments

Further to the above, Macau, China reported that it has updated its MAP guidance to include access to MAP in case of multilateral disputes, the multi-year resolution of recurring issues in MAP and suspension of tax collection during the period a MAP case is pending.

Basis for the peer review process

The peer review process entails an evaluation of Macau, China's implementation of the Action 14 Minimum Standard through an analysis of its legal and administrative framework relating to the mutual agreement procedure, as governed by its tax treaties, domestic legislation and regulations, as well as its MAP programme guidance (if any) and the practical application of that framework. The review process performed is desk-based and conducted through specific questionnaires completed by Macau, China, its peers and taxpayers. The questionnaires for the peer review process were sent to Macau, China and the peers on 30 August 2019.

The process consists of two stages: a peer review process (stage 1) and a peer monitoring process (stage 2). In stage 1, Macau, China's implementation of the Action 14 Minimum Standard as outlined above is evaluated, which has been reflected in a peer review report that has been adopted by the BEPS Inclusive Framework on 12 May 2020. This report identifies the strengths and shortcomings of Macau, China in relation to the implementation of this standard and provides for recommendations on how these shortcomings should be addressed. The stage 1 report is published on the website of the OECD.[2] Stage 2 is launched within one year upon the adoption of the peer review report by the BEPS Inclusive Framework through an update report by Macau, China. In this update report, Macau, China reflected (i) what steps it has already taken, or are to be taken, to address any of the shortcomings identified in the peer review report and (ii) any plans or changes to its legislative and/or administrative framework concerning the implementation of the Action 14 Minimum Standard. The update report forms the basis for the completion of the peer review process, which is reflected in this update to the stage 1 peer review report.

Outline of the treaty analysis

For the purpose of this report and the statistics below, in assessing whether Macau, China is compliant with the elements of the Action 14 Minimum Standard that relate to a specific treaty provision, the newly negotiated treaties or the treaties as modified by a protocol, as described above, were taken into account, even if it concerned a modification or a replacement of an existing treaty. Reference is made to Annex A for the overview of Macau, China's tax treaties regarding the mutual agreement procedure.

Timing of the process and input received from peers and taxpayers

Stage 1 of the peer review process for Macau, China was launched on 30 August 2019, with the sending of questionnaires to Macau, China and its peers. The FTA MAP Forum has approved the stage 1 peer review report of Macau, China in March 2020, with the subsequent approval by the BEPS Inclusive Framework on 12 May 2020. On 12 May 2021, Macau, China submitted its update report, which initiated stage 2 of the process.

The period for evaluating Macau, China's implementation of the Action 14 Minimum Standard for stage 1 ranged from 1 January 2016 to 31 August 2019 and formed the basis for the stage 1 peer review report. The period of review for stage 2 started on 1 September 2019 and depicts all developments as from that date until 30 April 2021.

No peer input was provided on Macau, China's implementation of the Action 14 Minimum Standard. This can be explained by the fact that Macau, China's competent authorities has never received a MAP request from a taxpayer or from another competent authority.

Input by Macau, China and co-operation throughout the process

Macau, China provided informative answers in its questionnaire. Macau, China was very responsive in the course of the drafting of the peer review report by responding timely and comprehensively to requests for additional information, and provided further clarity where necessary. In addition, Macau, China provided the following information:

- MAP profile[3]
- MAP statistics[4] according to the MAP Statistics Reporting Framework (see below).

During the stage 2 process, Macau, China submitted its update report on time and the information included was extensive. Macau, China was very co-operative during stage 2 and the finalisation of the peer review process.

Finally, Macau, China is a member of the FTA MAP Forum and has shown good co-operation during the peer review process.

Overview of MAP caseload in Macau, China

Macau, China has not been involved in any MAP cases during the period under review for stage 1 or stage 2.

General outline of the peer review report

This report includes an evaluation of Macau, China's implementation of the Action 14 Minimum Standard. The report comprises the following four sections:

A. Preventing disputes

B. Availability and access to MAP

C. Resolution of MAP cases

D. Implementation of MAP agreements.

Each of these sections is divided into elements of the Action 14 Minimum Standard, as described in the terms of reference to monitor and review the implementation of the BEPS Action 14 Minimum Standard to make dispute resolution mechanisms more effective ("**Terms of Reference**").[5] Apart from analysing Macau, China's legal framework and its administrative practice, the report also incorporates peer input and responses to such input by Macau, China during stage 1 and stage 2. Furthermore, the report depicts the changes adopted and plans shared by Macau, China to implement elements of the Action 14 Minimum Standard where relevant. The conclusion of each element identifies areas for improvement (if any) and provides for recommendations how the specific area for improvement should be addressed.

The basis of this report is the outcome of the stage 1 peer review process, which has identified in each element areas for improvement (if any) and provides for recommendations how the specific area for improvement should be addressed. Following the outcome of the peer monitoring process of stage 2, each of the elements have been updated with a recent development section to reflect any actions taken or changes made on how recommendations have been addressed, or to reflect other changes in the legal and administrative framework of Macau, China relating to the implementation of the Action 14 Minimum Standard. Where it concerns changes to MAP guidance or statistics, these changes are reflected in the analysis sections of the elements, with a general description of the changes included in the recent development sections.

The objective of the Action 14 Minimum Standard is to make dispute resolution mechanisms more effective and concerns a continuous effort. Where recommendations have been fully implemented, this has been reflected and the conclusion section of the relevant element has been modified accordingly, but Macau, China should continue to act in accordance with a given element of the Action 14 Minimum Standard, even if there is no area for improvement and recommendation for this specific element.

Notes

1. The tax treaties Macau, China has entered into are available at: www.dsf.gov.mo/. The treaties that are signed but have not yet entered into force are with Belgium (2006) and Cambodia (2021). Reference is made to Annex A for the overview of Macau, China's tax treaties concerning the mutual agreement procedure.

2. Available at: https://www.oecd.org/tax/beps/making-dispute-resolution-more-effective-map-peer-review-report-macau-china-stage-1-c5d34f2c-en.htm.

3. Available at: https://www.oecd.org/tax/dispute/Macau-Dispute-Resolution-Profile.pdf.

4. The MAP statistics of Macau, China are included in Annexes B and C of this report.

5. Terms of reference to monitor and review the implementing of the BEPS Action 14 Minimum Standard to make dispute resolution mechanisms more effective. Available at: www.oecd.org/tax/beps/beps-action-14-on-more-effective-dispute-resolution-peer-review-documents.pdf.

Part A

Preventing disputes

[A.1] Include Article 25(3), first sentence, of the OECD Model Tax Convention in tax treaties

> Jurisdictions should ensure that their tax treaties contain a provision which requires the competent authority of their jurisdiction to endeavour to resolve by mutual agreement any difficulties or doubts arising as to the interpretation or application of their tax treaties.

1. Cases may arise concerning the interpretation or the application of tax treaties that do not necessarily relate to individual cases, but are more of a general nature. Inclusion of the first sentence of Article 25(3) of the OECD Model Tax Convention (OECD, 2017a) in tax treaties invites and authorises competent authorities to solve these cases, which may avoid submission of MAP requests and/or future disputes from arising, and which may reinforce the consistent bilateral application of tax treaties.

Current situation of Macau, China's tax treaties

2. All of Macau, China's six tax treaties contain a provision equivalent to Article 25(3), first sentence, of the OECD Model Tax Convention (OECD, 2017a) requiring their competent authority to endeavour to resolve by mutual agreement any difficulties or doubts arising as to the interpretation or application of the tax treaty.

3. No peer input was provided during stage 1.

Recent developments

Bilateral modifications

4. Macau, China signed a new tax treaty with one treaty partner which is a newly negotiated treaty with a treaty partner with which there was no treaty yet in place. This treaty has not entered into force as yet. This treaty includes a provision that is equivalent to Article 25(3), first sentence, of the OECD Model Tax Convention (OECD, 2017a). The effect of this newly signed treaty has been reflected in the analysis above where it has relevance.

Peer input

5. No peer input was provided.

Anticipated modifications

6. Macau, China reported it will seek to include Article 25(3), first sentence, of the OECD Model Tax Convention (OECD, 2017a) in all of its future tax treaties.

Conclusion

	Areas for improvement	Recommendations
[A.1]	-	-

[A.2] Provide roll-back of bilateral APAs in appropriate cases

> Jurisdictions with bilateral advance pricing arrangement ("APA") programmes should provide for the roll-back of APAs in appropriate cases, subject to the applicable time limits (such as statutes of limitation for assessment) where the relevant facts and circumstances in the earlier tax years are the same and subject to the verification of these facts and circumstances on audit.

7. An APA is an arrangement that determines, in advance of controlled transactions, an appropriate set of criteria (e.g. method, comparables and appropriate adjustment thereto, critical assumptions as to future events) for the determination of the transfer pricing for those transactions over a fixed period of time[1]. The methodology to be applied prospectively under a bilateral or multilateral APA may be relevant in determining the treatment of comparable controlled transactions in previous filed years. The "roll-back" of an APA to these previous filed years may be helpful to prevent or resolve potential transfer pricing disputes.

Macau, China's APA programme

8. Macau, China has reported that it does not have an APA programme.

Roll-back of bilateral APAs

9. Since Macau, China does not have an APA programme in place, there is no possibility to provide roll-back of bilateral APAs to previous years.

Recent developments

10. There are no recent developments with respect to element A.2.

Practical application of roll-back of bilateral APAs

Period 1 January 2016-31 August 2019 (stage 1)

11. Macau, China reported not having received any requests for bilateral APAs in the period 1 January 2016-31 August 2019, which is logical given that Macau, China does not have such a programme in place.

12. No peer input was provided.

Period 1 September 2019-30 April 2021 (stage 2)

13. Macau, China reported also not having received any requests for a bilateral APA since 1 September 2019, which is logical given that Macau, China still does not have such a programme in place.

14. No peer input was provided.

Anticipated modifications

15. Macau, China indicated that it does not anticipate any modifications in relation to element A.2.

Conclusion

	Areas for improvement	Recommendations
[A.2]	-	-

Note

1. This description of an APA is based on the definition of an APA in the OECD Transfer Pricing Guidelines for Multinational Enterprises and Tax Administrations (OECD, 2017b).

References

OECD (2017a), *Model Tax Convention on Income and on Capital 2017 (Full Version)*, OECD Publishing, Paris, https://dx.doi.org/10.1787/g2g972ee-en.

OECD (2017b), *OECD Transfer Pricing Guidelines for Multinational Enterprises and Tax Administrations 2017*, https://dx.doi.org/10.1787/tpg-2017-en.

Part B

Availability and access to MAP

[B.1] Include Article 25(1) of the OECD Model Tax Convention in tax treaties

> Jurisdictions should ensure that their tax treaties contain a MAP provision which provides that when the taxpayer considers that the actions of one or both of the Contracting Parties result or will result for the taxpayer in taxation not in accordance with the provisions of the tax treaty, the taxpayer, may irrespective of the remedies provided by the domestic law of those Contracting Parties, make a request for MAP assistance, and that the taxpayer can present the request within a period of no less than three years from the first notification of the action resulting in taxation not in accordance with the provisions of the tax treaty.

16. For resolving cases of taxation not in accordance with the provisions of the tax treaty, it is necessary that tax treaties include a provision allowing taxpayers to request a mutual agreement procedure and that this procedure can be requested irrespective of the remedies provided by the domestic law of the treaty partners. In addition, to provide certainty to taxpayers and competent authorities on the availability of the mutual agreement procedure, a minimum period of three years for submission of a MAP request, beginning on the date of the first notification of the action resulting in taxation not in accordance with the provisions of the tax treaty, is the baseline.

Current situation of Macau, China's tax treaties

Inclusion of Article 25(1), first sentence of the OECD Model Tax Convention

17. One out of Macau, China's six tax treaties contains a provision equivalent to Article 25(1), first sentence, of the OECD Model Tax Convention (OECD, 2017), as amended by the Action 14 final report (OECD, 2015b) and allowing taxpayers to submit a MAP request to the competent authority of either state when they consider that the actions of one or both of the treaty partners result or will result for the taxpayer in taxation not in accordance with the provisions of the tax treaty and that can be requested irrespective of the remedies provided by domestic law of either state. Furthermore, three of these six treaties contain a provision equivalent to Article 25(1), first sentence, of the OECD Model Tax Convention (OECD, 2015a) as it read prior to the adoption of the Action 14 final report (OECD, 2015b), allowing taxpayers to submit a MAP request to the competent authority of the state in which they are resident.

18. The remaining two treaties are considered not to have the full equivalent of Article 25(1), first sentence, of the OECD Model Tax Convention (OECD, 2015a) as it read prior to the adoption of the Action 14 final report (OECD, 2015b), since taxpayers are not allowed to submit a MAP request in the state of which they are a national where the case

comes under the non-discrimination article. However, since the non-discrimination provision of one of these two tax treaties only covers nationals that are resident of one of the contracting states, one of those two treaties is considered to be in line with this part of element B.1.

19. For the remaining treaty, the non-discrimination provision is almost identical to Article 24(1) of the OECD Model Tax Convention (OECD, 2017) and applies both to nationals that are and are not resident of one of the contracting states. The omission of the full text of Article 25(1), first sentence, of the OECD Model Tax Convention (OECD, 2015a), as it read prior to the adoption of the Action 14 final report (OECD, 2015b) is therefore not clarified by the absence of or a limited scope of the non-discrimination provision, following which the treaty is considered to not be in line with this part of element B.1.

Inclusion of Article 25(1), second sentence of the OECD Model Tax Convention

20. All of Macau, China's six tax treaties contain a provision equivalent to Article 25(1), second sentence, of the OECD Model Tax Convention (OECD, 2017) allowing taxpayers to submit a MAP request within a period of no less than three years from the first notification of the action resulting in taxation not in accordance with the provisions of the particular tax treaty.

Peer input

21. No peer input was provided during stage 1.

Practical application

Article 25(1), first sentence, of the OECD Model Tax Convention

22. As follows from the analysis in paragraphs 17-19 above, all of Macau, China's tax treaties allow the filing of a MAP request irrespective of domestic remedies. In this respect, Macau, China indicated that nothing in its domestic tax law prevents a taxpayer from requesting MAP assistance where the taxpayer has sought to resolve the issue under dispute via the judicial and administrative remedies provided under its domestic law. However, where domestic judicial remedies have been concluded, Macau, China indicated that its competent authority would be bound by the decision in such remedies and therefore, it will only seek to resolve the MAP case by having the treaty partner providing for correlative relief in line with the decision of the court. This is confirmed in section 6 of Macau, China's MAP guidance.

Recent developments

Bilateral modifications

23. Macau, China signed a new tax treaty with one treaty partner which is a newly negotiated treaty with a treaty partner with which there was no treaty yet in place. This treaty is yet to enter into force. The treaty includes Article 25(1), first and second sentence, of the OECD Model Tax Convention (OECD, 2017) as amended by the Action 14 final report (OECD, 2015b). The effect of this newly signed treaty has been reflected in the analysis above where it has relevance.

Other developments

24. Macau, China reported that for the tax treaty that does not contain the equivalent of Article 25(1), first sentence, of the OECD Model Tax Convention (OECD, 2015a) as it

read prior to the adoption of the Action 14 final report (OECD, 2015b), negotiations on an amending protocol have been initiated and are ongoing.

Peer input

25.   No peer input was provided.

Anticipated modifications

26.   Macau, China reported it will seek to include Article 25(1) of the OECD Model Tax Convention (OECD, 2017) as amended by the Action 14 final report (OECD, 2015b), in all of its future tax treaties.

Conclusion

	Areas for improvement	Recommendations
[B.1]	One out of six tax treaties does not contain a provision that is equivalent to Article 25(1), first sentence, of the OECD Model Tax Convention (OECD, 2015a), either as it read prior to the adoption of the Action 14 final report or as amended by that report (OECD, 2015b). With respect to this treaty, negotiations are ongoing.	For the treaty that does not contain the equivalent of Article 25(1) of the OECD Model Tax Convention (OECD, 2015a), as it read prior to the adoption of the Action 14 final report (OECD, 2015b), Macau, China should continue negotiations with the treaty partner with a view to including the required provision. This concerns a provision that is equivalent to Article 25(1), first sentence of the OECD Model Tax Convention (OECD, 2015a) either: a. as amended in the Action 14 final report (OECD, 2015b); or b. as it read prior to the adoption of the Action 14 final report (OECD, 2015b), thereby including the full sentence of such provision.

[B.2]   **Allow submission of MAP requests to the competent authority of either treaty partner, or, alternatively, introduce a bilateral consultation or notification process**

> Jurisdictions should ensure that either (i) their tax treaties contain a provision which provides that the taxpayer can make a request for MAP assistance to the competent authority of either Contracting Party, or (ii) where the treaty does not permit a MAP request to be made to either Contracting Party and the competent authority who received the MAP request from the taxpayer does not consider the taxpayer's objection to be justified, the competent authority should implement a bilateral consultation or notification process which allows the other competent authority to provide its views on the case (such consultation shall not be interpreted as consultation as to how to resolve the case).

27.   In order to ensure that all competent authorities concerned are aware of MAP requests submitted, for a proper consideration of the request by them and to ensure that taxpayers have effective access to MAP in eligible cases, it is essential that all tax treaties contain a provision that either allows taxpayers to submit a MAP request to the competent authority:

i.   of either treaty partner; or, in the absence of such provision,

ii. where it is a resident, or to the competent authority of the state of which they are a national if their cases come under the non-discrimination article. In such cases, jurisdictions should have in place a bilateral consultation or notification process where a competent authority considers the objection raised by the taxpayer in a MAP request as being not justified.

Domestic bilateral consultation or notification process in place

28. As discussed under element B.1, out of Macau, China's six treaties, one currently contains a provision equivalent to Article 25(1), first sentence, of the OECD Model Tax Convention (OECD, 2017), as amended by the Action 14 final report (OECD, 2015b), allowing taxpayers to submit a MAP request to the competent authority of either treaty partner.

29. Macau, China reported that it has introduced a bilateral notification process that allows the other competent authority concerned to provide its views on the case when Macau, China's competent authority considers the objection raised in the MAP request not to be justified.

30. In this regard, section 5 of Macau, China's MAP guidance clarifies that within 30 days from the date of receipt of a MAP request (even if the request is not accepted or remains pending), Macau, China's competent authority will inform the competent authority of the concerned treaty partner, providing a copy of the request and of all the documents attached hereto. Macau, China's internal guidelines also outline this process and the template for notification of filed MAP requests to the treaty partner's competent authority where the objection raised by a taxpayer is considered not justified is attached as an annex to the internal guidelines.

Recent developments

31. There are no recent developments with respect to element B.2.

Practical application

Period 1 January 2016-31 August 2019 (stage 1)

32. Macau, China reported that in the period 1 January 2016-31 January 2019 its competent authority has not received any MAP requests. Therefore, there were no cases where it was decided that the objection raised by taxpayers in such request was not justified.

33. No peer input was provided.

Period 1 September 2019-30 April 2021 (stage 2)

34. Macau, China reported that also since 1 September 2019, its competent authority has not received any MAP requests. Therefore, there were no cases where it was decided that the objection raised by taxpayers in such request was not justified.

35. No peer input was provided.

Anticipated modifications

36. Macau, China indicated that it does not anticipate any modifications in relation to element B.2.

Conclusion

	Areas for improvement	Recommendations
[B.2]	-	-

[B.3] Provide access to MAP in transfer pricing cases

> Jurisdictions should provide access to MAP in transfer pricing cases.

37. Where two or more tax administrations take different positions on what constitutes arm's length conditions for specific transactions between associated enterprises, economic double taxation may occur. Not granting access to MAP with respect to a treaty partner's transfer pricing adjustment, with a view to eliminating the economic double taxation that may arise from such adjustment, will likely frustrate the main objective of tax treaties. Jurisdictions should thus provide access to MAP in transfer pricing cases.

Legal and administrative framework

38. All of Macau, China's six tax treaties contain a provision equivalent to Article 9(2) of the OECD Model Tax Convention (OECD, 2017) requiring their state to make a correlative adjustment in case a transfer pricing adjustment is imposed by the treaty partner.

39. Access to MAP should be provided in transfer pricing cases regardless of whether the equivalent of Article 9(2) is contained in Macau, China's tax treaties and irrespective of whether its domestic legislation enables the granting of corresponding adjustments. In accordance with element B3, as translated from the Action 14 Minimum Standard, Macau, China indicated that it will always provide access to MAP for transfer pricing cases and is willing to make corresponding adjustments. Section 2 of Macau, China's MAP guidance indicates that transfer pricing cases are considered cases that are eligible for MAP in Macau, China.

Recent developments

Bilateral modifications

40. Macau, China signed a new tax treaty with one treaty partner which is a newly negotiated treaty with a treaty partner with which there was no treaty yet in place. This treaty has not entered into force as yet. This treaty includes a provision that is equivalent to Article 9(2) of the OECD Model Tax Convention (OECD, 2017). The effect of this newly signed treaty has been reflected in the analysis above where it has relevance.

Application of legal and administrative framework in practice

Period 1 January 2016-31 August 2019 (stage 1)

41. Macau, China reported that in the period 1 January 2016-31 August 2019, it has not received any MAP requests and therefore has not denied access to MAP on the basis that the case concerned a transfer pricing case.

42. No peer input was provided.

Period 1 September 2019-30 April 2021 (stage 2)

43. Macau, China reported that also since 1 September 2019, it has not received any MAP requests and therefore has not denied access to MAP on the basis that the case concerned a transfer pricing case.

44. No peer input was provided.

Anticipated modifications

45. Macau, China reported that it is in favour of including Article 9(2) of the OECD Model Tax Convention (OECD, 2017) in its tax treaties where possible and that it will seek to include Article 9(2) in all of its future tax treaties. Other than this, Macau, China did not indicate that it anticipates any modifications in relation to element B.3.

Conclusion

	Areas for improvement	Recommendations
[B.3]	-	-

[B.4] Provide access to MAP in relation to the application of anti-abuse provisions

> Jurisdictions should provide access to MAP in cases in which there is a disagreement between the taxpayer and the tax authorities making the adjustment as to whether the conditions for the application of a treaty anti-abuse provision have been met or as to whether the application of a domestic law anti-abuse provision is in conflict with the provisions of a treaty.

46. There is no general rule denying access to MAP in cases of perceived abuse. In order to protect taxpayers from arbitrary application of anti-abuse provisions in tax treaties and in order to ensure that competent authorities have a common understanding on such application, it is important that taxpayers have access to MAP if they consider the interpretation and/or application of a treaty anti-abuse provision as being incorrect. Subsequently, to avoid cases in which the application of domestic anti-abuse legislation is in conflict with the provisions of a tax treaty, it is also important that taxpayers have access to MAP in such cases.

Legal and administrative framework

47. None of Macau, China's six tax treaties allows competent authorities to restrict access to MAP for cases where a treaty anti-abuse provision applies or where there is a disagreement between the taxpayer and the tax authorities as to whether the application of a domestic law anti-abuse provision is in conflict with the provisions of a tax treaty. In addition, the domestic law and/or administrative processes of Macau, China do not include a provision allowing its competent authority to limit access to MAP for cases in which there is a disagreement between the taxpayer and the tax authorities as to whether the conditions for the application of a domestic law anti-abuse provision is in conflict with the provisions of a tax treaty.

48. Section 2 of Macau, China's MAP guidance clarifies that there is no restriction on a taxpayer's access to MAP for cases where the taxpayer and the tax authorities that have made an adjustment do not agree as to whether the conditions of the application of an

anti-abuse provision of a tax treaty have been met and whether the application of anti-abuse provision of an internal law is in conflict with the provision of a tax treaty.

Recent developments

49. There are no recent developments with respect to element B.4.

Practical application

Period 1 January 2016-31 August 2019 (stage 1)

50. Macau. China reported that in the period 1 January 2016-31 August 2019, Macau, China's competent authority has not received any MAP requests and therefore, has not denied access to MAP in cases in which there was a disagreement between the taxpayer and the tax authorities as to whether the conditions for the application of a treaty anti-abuse provision have been met, or as to whether the application of a domestic law anti-abuse provision is in conflict with the provisions of a tax treaty.

51. No peer input was provided.

Period 1 September 2019-30 April 2021 (stage 2)

52. Macau, China reported that also since 1 September 2019, its competent authority has not received any MAP requests and therefore, has not denied access to MAP in cases in which there was a disagreement between the taxpayer and the tax authorities as to whether the conditions for the application of a treaty anti-abuse provision have been met, or as to whether the application of a domestic law anti-abuse provision is in conflict with the provisions of a tax treaty.

53. No peer input was provided.

Anticipated modifications

54. Macau, China indicated that it does not anticipate any modifications in relation to element B.4.

Conclusion

	Areas for improvement	Recommendations
[B.4]	-	-

[B.5] Provide access to MAP in cases of audit settlements

> Jurisdictions should not deny access to MAP in cases where there is an audit settlement between tax authorities and taxpayers. If jurisdictions have an administrative or statutory dispute settlement/resolution process independent from the audit and examination functions and that can only be accessed through a request by the taxpayer, jurisdictions may limit access to the MAP with respect to the matters resolved through that process.

55. An audit settlement procedure can be valuable to taxpayers by providing certainty on their tax position. Nevertheless, as double taxation may not be fully eliminated by agreeing on such settlements, taxpayers should have access to the MAP in such cases, unless they

were already resolved via an administrative or statutory disputes settlement/resolution process that functions independently from the audit and examination function and which is only accessible through a request by taxpayers.

Legal and administrative framework

Audit settlements

56. Macau, China reported that there is no audit settlement process available in Macau, China.

Administrative or statutory dispute settlement/resolution process

57. Macau, China reported it does not have an administrative or statutory dispute settlement/resolution process that limits access to MAP in place, which is independent from the audit and examination functions and which can only be accessed through a request by the taxpayer.

Recent developments

58. There are no recent developments with respect to element B.5.

Practical application

Period 1 January 2016-31 August 2019 (stage 1)

59. Macau, China reported that in the period 1 January 2016-31 August 2019 it has not denied access to MAP in any case where the issue presented by the taxpayer in a MAP request has already been resolved through an audit settlement between the taxpayer and the tax administration, which is explained by the fact that such settlements are not possible in Macau, China.

60. No peer input was provided.

Period 1 September 2019-30 April 2021 (stage 2)

61. Macau, China reported that since 1 September 2019 it has also not denied access to MAP for cases where the issue presented by the taxpayer has already been dealt with in an audit settlement between the taxpayer and the tax administration since such settlements are still not possible in Macau, China.

62. No peer input was provided.

Anticipated modifications

63. Macau, China indicated that it does not anticipate any modifications in relation to element B.5.

Conclusion

	Areas for improvement	Recommendations
[B.5]	-	-

[B.6] Provide access to MAP if required information is submitted

> Jurisdictions should not limit access to MAP based on the argument that insufficient information was provided if the taxpayer has provided the required information based on the rules, guidelines and procedures made available to taxpayers on access to and the use of MAP.

64. To resolve cases where there is taxation not in accordance with the provisions of the tax treaty, it is important that competent authorities do not limit access to MAP when taxpayers have complied with the information and documentation requirements as provided in the jurisdiction's guidance relating hereto. Access to MAP will be facilitated when such required information and documentation is made publicly available.

Legal framework on access to MAP and information to be submitted

65. The information and documentation Macau, China requires taxpayers to include in a request for MAP assistance are discussed under element B.8.

66. Macau, China reported that when the competent authority receives a MAP request that does not include all the information and documentation required to be submitted pursuant to Macau, China's MAP guidance, the taxpayers have to submit additional information requested within 30 days. This is clarified in section 5 of Macau, China's MAP guidance. Macau, China further reported that its competent authority may, at its discretion, provide for a further extension of 30 days to allow the taxpayer to submit the missing additional information.

Recent developments

67. There are no recent developments with respect to element B.6.

Practical application

Period 1 January 2016-31 August 2019 (stage 1)

68. Macau, China reported that it provides access to MAP in all cases where taxpayers have complied with the information or documentation requirements as set out in its MAP guidance. It further reported that in the period 1 January 2016-31 August 2019 its competent authority has not denied access to MAP for cases where the taxpayer had not provided the required information or documentation, which can be clarified by the fact that no MAP cases have arisen in Macau, China during this period.

69. No peer input was provided.

Period 1 September 2019-30 April 2021 (stage 2)

70. Macau, China reported that since 1 September 2019 its competent authority has also not denied access to MAP for cases where the taxpayer had provided the required information or documentation, which can be clarified by the fact that no MAP cases have arisen in Macau, China since this date either.

71. No peer input was provided.

Anticipated modifications

72. Macau, China indicated that it does not anticipate any modifications in relation to element B.6.

Conclusion

	Areas for improvement	Recommendations
[B.6]	-	-

[B.7] Include Article 25(3), second sentence, of the OECD Model Tax Convention in tax treaties

> Jurisdictions should ensure that their tax treaties contain a provision under which competent authorities may consult together for the elimination of double taxation in cases not provided for in their tax treaties.

73. For ensuring that tax treaties operate effectively and in order for competent authorities to be able to respond quickly to unanticipated situations, it is useful that tax treaties include the second sentence of Article 25(3) of the OECD Model Tax Convention (OECD, 2017), enabling them to consult together for the elimination of double taxation in cases not provided for by these treaties.

Current situation of Macau, China's tax treaties

74. Out of Macau, China's six tax treaties, five contain a provision equivalent to Article 25(3), second sentence, of the OECD Model Tax Convention (OECD, 2017) allowing their competent authorities to consult together for the elimination of double taxation in cases not provided for in their tax treaties. The remaining treaty does not contain a provision that is based on or equivalent to Article 25(3), second sentence, of the OECD Model Tax Convention (OECD, 2017).

75. No peer input was provided during stage 1.

Recent developments

Bilateral modifications

76. Macau, China signed a new tax treaty with one treaty partner which is a newly negotiated treaty with a treaty partner with which there was no treaty yet in place. This treaty has not entered into force as yet. This treaty includes a provision that is equivalent to Article 25(3), second sentence, of the OECD Model Tax Convention (OECD, 2017). The effect of this newly signed treaty has been reflected in the analysis above where it has relevance.

Other developments

77. Macau, China reported that for the tax treaty that does not contain the equivalent of Article 25(3), second sentence, of the OECD Model Tax Convention (OECD, 2017), negotiations are scheduled to be initiated once ongoing negotiations are completed.

Peer input

78. No peer input was provided.

Anticipated modifications

79. Macau, China reported it will seek to include Article 25(3), second sentence, of the OECD Model Tax Convention (OECD, 2017) in all of its future tax treaties.

Conclusion

	Areas for improvement	Recommendations
[B.7]	One out of six tax treaties does not contain a provision that is equivalent to Article 25(3), second sentence, of the OECD Model Tax Convention (OECD, 2017). With respect to this treaty, negotiations are envisaged.	For the treaty that does not contain the equivalent of Article 25(3), second sentence, of the OECD Model Tax Convention (OECD, 2017), Macau, China should continue (the initiation of) negotiations with the treaty partner with a view to including the required provision.

[B.8] Publish clear and comprehensive MAP guidance

> Jurisdictions should publish clear rules, guidelines and procedures on access to and use of the MAP and include the specific information and documentation that should be submitted in a taxpayer's request for MAP assistance.

80. Information on a jurisdiction's MAP regime facilitates the timely initiation and resolution of MAP cases. Clear rules, guidelines and procedures on access to and use of the MAP are essential for making taxpayers and other stakeholders aware of how a jurisdiction's MAP regime functions. In addition, to ensure that a MAP request is received and will be reviewed by the competent authority in a timely manner, it is important that a jurisdiction's MAP guidance clearly and comprehensively explains how a taxpayer can make a MAP request and what information and documentation should be included in such request.

Macau, China's MAP guidance

81. Macau, China has issued rules, guidelines and procedures on the mutual agreement procedure, which was last updated in June 2021 and is available (in English) at:

www.dsf.gov.mo/download/tax/E_MAPGuidelines.pdf

82. Macau, China's MAP guidance comprises seven parts, which deal with the following topics:

i. Introduction

ii. Scope of the Mutual Agreement Procedure

iii. Who can request to initiate a Mutual Agreement Procedure

iv. How to initiate a Mutual Agreement Procedure

v. Processing a Mutual Agreement Procedure

vi. Implementation of the Agreement reached under a Mutual Agreement Procedure

vii. The Mutual Agreement Procedure and Macao legislation.

83. These sections cover the following information:

a. contact information of the competent authority or the office in charge of MAP cases

b. the manner and form in which the taxpayer should submit its MAP request

c. the specific information and documentation that should be included in a MAP request

d. how the MAP functions in terms of timing and the role of the competent authorities

e. relationship with domestic available remedies

f. access to MAP in transfer pricing cases, anti-abuse provisions, bona fide foreign-initiated self-adjustments, multilateral disputes

g. the multi-year resolution of recurring issues through MAP

h. implementation of MAP agreements (including the steps of the process and the timing of such steps for the implementation of MAP agreements, and any actions to be taken by taxpayers)

i. rights and role of taxpayers in the process

j. suspension of tax collection for the period a MAP case is pending

k. interest charges and penalties.

84. The above-described MAP guidance of Macau, China includes detailed information on the availability and the use of MAP and how its competent authority conducts the procedure in practice. This guidance includes the information that the FTA MAP Forum agreed should be included in a jurisdiction's MAP guidance, which concerns: (i) contact information of the competent authority or the office in charge of MAP cases and (ii) the manner and form in which the taxpayer should submit its MAP request.[1]

Information and documentation to be included in a MAP request

85. To facilitate the review of a MAP request by competent authorities and to have more consistency in the required content of MAP requests, the FTA MAP Forum agreed on guidance that jurisdictions could use in their domestic guidance on what information and documentation taxpayers need to include in a request for MAP assistance.[2] This agreed guidance is shown below. Macau, China's MAP guidance enumerating which items must be included in a request for MAP assistance are checked in the following list:

- ☑ identity of the taxpayer(s) covered in the MAP request
- ☑ the basis for the request
- ☑ facts of the case
- ☑ analysis of the issue(s) requested to be resolved via MAP
- ☑ whether the MAP request was also submitted to the competent authority of the other treaty partner
- ☑ whether the MAP request was also submitted to another authority under another instrument that provides for a mechanism to resolve treaty-related disputes
- ☑ whether the issue(s) involved were dealt with previously

☑ a statement confirming that all information and documentation provided in the MAP request is accurate and that the taxpayer will assist the competent authority in its resolution of the issue(s) presented in the MAP request by furnishing any other information or documentation required by the competent authority in a timely manner.

86. In addition to the above, Macau, China's MAP guidance also requires that taxpayers provide:

a. the treaty partner jurisdiction and tax periods involved

b. a statement committing to answer as completely and swiftly as possible all reasonable and appropriate requests made by Macau China's competent authority and to have all relevant documentation at the disposal of the competent authority.

Recent developments

87. Macau, China reported that since 1 September 2019, it has updated its MAP guidance to reflect the following:

a. access to MAP would be granted for multilateral disputes

b. taxpayers may request for the multi-year resolution of recurring issues through MAP

c. the possibility of suspension of tax collection during the course of a MAP.

Anticipated modifications

88. Macau, China indicated that it does not anticipate any modifications in relation to element B.8.

Conclusion

	Areas for improvement	Recommendations
[B.8]	-	-

[B.9] Make MAP guidance available and easily accessible and publish MAP profile

> Jurisdictions should take appropriate measures to make rules, guidelines and procedures on access to and use of the MAP available and easily accessible to the public and should publish their jurisdiction MAP profiles on a shared public platform pursuant to the agreed template.

89. The public availability and accessibility of a jurisdiction's MAP guidance increases public awareness on access to and the use of the MAP in that jurisdiction. Publishing MAP profiles on a shared public platform further promotes the transparency and dissemination of the MAP programme.[3]

Rules, guidelines and procedures on access to and use of the MAP

90. The MAP guidance of Macau, China is published and can be found (in English) at:

www.dsf.gov.mo/download/tax/E_MAPGuidelines.pdf

91. This guidance was last updated in June 2021. As regards its accessibility, Macau, China's MAP guidance can easily be found on the website of the Financial Services Bureau website with a direct link available on the home page. It can also be easily found by searching for "Macau, China mutual agreement procedure" on a search engine.

MAP profile

92. The MAP profile of Macau, China is published on the website of the OECD and was last updated in June 2021. This MAP profile is complete and often with detailed information. This profile includes external links that provide extra information and guidance where appropriate.

Recent developments

93. Apart from the fact that Macau, China updated its MAP profile published on the website of the OECD, there are no recent developments with respect to element B.9.

Anticipated modifications

94. Macau, China indicated that it does not anticipate any modifications in relation to element B.9.

Conclusion

	Areas for improvement	Recommendations
[B.9]	-	-

[B.10] Clarify in MAP guidance that audit settlements do not preclude access to MAP

> Jurisdictions should clarify in their MAP guidance that audit settlements between tax authorities and taxpayers do not preclude access to MAP. If jurisdictions have an administrative or statutory dispute settlement/resolution process independent from the audit and examination functions and that can only be accessed through a request by the taxpayer, and jurisdictions limit access to the MAP with respect to the matters resolved through that process, jurisdictions should notify their treaty partners of such administrative or statutory processes and should expressly address the effects of those processes with respect to the MAP in their public guidance on such processes and in their public MAP programme guidance.

95. As explained under element B.5, an audit settlement can be valuable to taxpayers by providing certainty to them on their tax position. Nevertheless, as double taxation may not be fully eliminated by agreeing with such settlements, it is important that a jurisdiction's MAP guidance clarifies that in case of audit settlement taxpayers have access to the MAP. In addition, for providing clarity on the relationship between administrative or statutory dispute settlement or resolution processes and the MAP (if any), it is critical that both the public guidance on such processes and the public MAP programme guidance address the effects of those processes, if any. Finally, as the MAP represents a collaborative approach between treaty partners, it is helpful that treaty partners are notified of each other's MAP programme and limitations thereto, particularly in relation to the previously mentioned processes.

MAP and audit settlements in the MAP guidance

96. As previously discussed under B.5, audit settlements are not possible in Macau, China. The relationship between access to MAP and audit settlements made between taxpayers and another jurisdiction is described in Section 7 of Macau, China's MAP guidance.

97. No peer input was provided.

MAP and other administrative or statutory dispute settlement/resolution processes in available guidance

98. As previously mentioned under element B.5, Macau, China does not have an administrative or statutory dispute settlement/resolution process that limits access to MAP in place that is independent from the audit and examination functions and that can only be accessed through a request by the taxpayer. In that regard, there is no need to address the effects of such process with respect to MAP in Macau, China's MAP guidance.

99. No peer input was provided.

Notification of treaty partners of existing administrative or statutory dispute settlement/resolution processes

100. As Macau, China does not have an internal administrative or statutory dispute settlement/resolution process that limits access to MAP in place, there is no need for notifying treaty partners of such process.

Recent developments

101. There are no recent developments with respect to element B.10.

Anticipated modifications

102. Macau, China indicated that it does not anticipate any modifications in relation to element B.10.

Conclusion

	Areas for improvement	Recommendations
[B.10]	-	-

Notes

1. Available at: www.oecd.org/tax/beps/beps-action-14-on-more-effective-dispute-resolution-peer-review-documents.pdf.
2. Idem.
3. The shared public platform can be found at: www.oecd.org/ctp/dispute/country-map-profiles.htm.

References

OECD (2015a), *Model Tax Convention on Income and on Capital 2014 (Full Version)*, OECD Publishing, Paris, https://dx.doi.org/10.1787/9789264239081-en.

OECD (2015b), "Making Dispute Resolution Mechanisms More Effective, Action 14 – 2015 Final Report", in *OECD/G20 Base Erosion and Profit Shifting Project*, OECD Publishing, Paris, https://dx.doi.org/10.1787/9789264241633-en.

OECD (2017), *Model Tax Convention on Income and on Capital 2017 (Full Version)*, OECD Publishing, Paris, https://dx.doi.org/10.1787/g2g972ee-en.

Part C

Resolution of MAP cases

[C.1] Include Article 25(2), first sentence, of the OECD Model Tax Convention in tax treaties

> Jurisdictions should ensure that their tax treaties contain a provision which requires that the competent authority who receives a MAP request from the taxpayer, shall endeavour, if the objection from the taxpayer appears to be justified and the competent authority is not itself able to arrive at a satisfactory solution, to resolve the MAP case by mutual agreement with the competent authority of the other Contracting Party, with a view to the avoidance of taxation which is not in accordance with the tax treaty.

103. It is of critical importance that in addition to allowing taxpayers to request for a MAP, tax treaties also include the equivalent of the first sentence of Article 25(2) of the OECD Model Tax Convention (OECD, 2017), which obliges competent authorities, in situations where the objection raised by taxpayers are considered justified and where cases cannot be unilaterally resolved, to enter into discussions with each other to resolve cases of taxation not in accordance with the provisions of a tax treaty.

Current situation of Macau, China's tax treaties

104. All of Macau, China's six tax treaties contain a provision equivalent to Article 25(2), first sentence, of the OECD Model Tax Convention (OECD, 2017) requiring its competent authority to endeavour – when the objection raised is considered justified and no unilateral solution is possible – to resolve by mutual agreement with the competent authority of the other treaty partner the MAP case with a view to the avoidance of taxation which is not in accordance with the tax treaty.

105. No peer input was provided during stage 1.

Recent developments

Bilateral modifications

106. Macau, China signed a new tax treaty with one treaty partner which is a newly negotiated treaty with a treaty partner with which there was no treaty yet in place. This treaty has not entered into force as yet. This treaty includes a provision that is equivalent to Article 25(2), first sentence, of the OECD Model Tax Convention (OECD, 2017). The effect of this newly signed treaty has been reflected in the analysis above where it has relevance.

Peer input

107. No peer input was provided.

Anticipated modifications

108. Macau, China reported it will seek to include Article 25(2), first sentence, of the OECD Model Tax Convention (OECD, 2017) in all of its future tax treaties.

Conclusion

	Areas for improvement	Recommendations
[C.1]	-	-

[C.2] **Seek to resolve MAP cases within a 24-month average timeframe**

> Jurisdictions should seek to resolve MAP cases within an average time frame of 24 months. This time frame applies to both jurisdictions (i.e. the jurisdiction which receives the MAP request from the taxpayer and its treaty partner).

109. As double taxation creates uncertainties and leads to costs for both taxpayers and jurisdictions, and as the resolution of MAP cases may also avoid (potential) similar issues for future years concerning the same taxpayers, it is important that MAP cases are resolved swiftly. A period of 24 months is considered as an appropriate time period to resolve MAP cases on average.

Reporting of MAP statistics

110. The FTA MAP Forum has agreed on rules for reporting of MAP statistics ("**MAP Statistics Reporting Framework**") for MAP requests submitted on or after 1 January 2016 ("**post-2015 cases**"). Also, for MAP requests submitted prior to that date ("**pre-2016 cases**"), the FTA MAP Forum agreed to report MAP statistics on the basis of an agreed template. Macau, China provided MAP statistics for 2016-20 pursuant to the MAP Statistics Reporting Framework within the given deadline. As Macau, China has not been involved in any MAP cases, it was not necessary to match its statistics with its treaty partners.

Monitoring of MAP statistics

111. As Macau, China has never been involved in a MAP case, it has no system in place that communicates, monitors and manages with its treaty partners the MAP caseload.

Analysis of Macau, China's MAP caseload

112. Macau, China has not been involved in any MAP cases during the Statistics Reporting Period.

Overview of cases closed during the Statistics Reporting Period

113. Macau, China has not been involved in any MAP cases during the Statistics Reporting Period.

Average timeframe needed to resolve MAP cases

114. Macau, China has not been involved in any MAP cases during the Statistics Reporting Period.

Peer input

115. No peer input was provided.

Recent developments

116. There are no recent developments with respect to element C.2.

Anticipated modifications

117. Macau, China indicated that it does not anticipate any modifications in relation to element C.2.

Conclusion

	Areas for improvement	Recommendations
[C.2]	-	-

[C.3] Provide adequate resources to the MAP function

> Jurisdictions should ensure that adequate resources are provided to the MAP function.

118. Adequate resources, including personnel, funding and training, are necessary to properly perform the competent authority function and to ensure that MAP cases are resolved in a timely, efficient and effective manner.

Description of Macau, China's competent authority

119. Under Macau, China's tax treaties, the competent authority function is assigned to the Chief Executive of Macau or his authorised representative. Macau, China reported that this function has been delegated to the Director of the Financial Services Bureau. Macau, China reported that its competent authority employs four staff members to deal with MAP cases as and when they arise, who are currently in charge of treaty negotiations. Macau, China also noted that these staff members are not responsible for audits and assessment.

120. Macau, China further reported that to date it considers the resources available to the competent authority to be sufficient given the fact that it has not received any MAP requests from taxpayers or other competent authorities.

Monitoring mechanism

121. As discussed under element C.2, Macau, China has not been involved in any MAP cases during the Statistics Reporting Period, so it does not have a monitoring mechanisms of available resources at this point.

122. Macau, China reported that there would be ongoing monitoring to guarantee that the Financial Services Bureau has sufficient human, financial and other resources to meet its obligations under the tax treaties and make sure that Macau, China has an effective MAP programme, while it considers that the resources allocated at present are sufficient given the amount of upcoming MAP requests expected.

Recent developments

123. There are no recent developments with respect to element C.3.

Practical application

MAP statistics

124. As discussed under element C.2, Macau, China's competent authority has not yet been involved in any MAP cases during the Statistics Reporting Period.

Peer input

125. No peer input was provided.

Anticipated modifications

126. Macau, China indicated that it does not anticipate any modifications in relation to element C.3.

Conclusion

	Areas for improvement	Recommendations
[C.3]	-	-

[C.4] Ensure staff in charge of MAP has the authority to resolve cases in accordance with the applicable tax treaty

> Jurisdictions should ensure that the staff in charge of MAP processes have the authority to resolve MAP cases in accordance with the terms of the applicable tax treaty, in particular without being dependent on the approval or the direction of the tax administration personnel who made the adjustments at issue or being influenced by considerations of the policy that the jurisdictions would like to see reflected in future amendments to the treaty.

127. Ensuring that staff in charge of MAP can and will resolve cases, absent any approval/direction by the tax administration personnel directly involved in the adjustment and absent any policy considerations, contributes to a principled and consistent approach to MAP cases.

Functioning of staff in charge of MAP

128. Macau, China reported that the staff members in its competent authority are in charge of tax negotiations, but are not involved in or responsible for tax audits and assessments, in order to ensure the effectiveness and independence of the MAP programme. Macau, China also reported that staff in charge of MAP cases will take into consideration the actual terms of a tax treaty as applicable for the relevant year and that it is committed not to be

influenced by policy considerations that Macau, China would like to see reflected in future amendments to the treaty.

129. With regard to the above, Macau, China considers that staff in charge of MAP has the necessary authority to resolve MAP cases and are not dependent on the approval/direction of outside personnel and that there are no impediments in Macau, China's abilities to perform its MAP functions.

Recent developments

130. There are no recent developments with respect to element C.4.

Practical application

131. No peer input was provided.

Anticipated modifications

132. Macau, China indicated that it does not anticipate any modifications in relation to element C.4.

Conclusion

	Areas for improvement	Recommendations
[C.4]	-	-

[C.5] Use appropriate performance indicators for the MAP function

> Jurisdictions should not use performance indicators for their competent authority functions and staff in charge of MAP processes based on the amount of sustained audit adjustments or maintaining tax revenue.

133. For ensuring that each case is considered on its individual merits and will be resolved in a principled and consistent manner, it is essential that any performance indicators for the competent authority function and for the staff in charge of MAP processes are appropriate and not based on the amount of sustained audit adjustments or aim at maintaining a certain amount of tax revenue.

Performance indicators used by Macau, China

134. Macau, China reported that there are standardised performance evaluation criteria for civil servants: effectiveness; sense of responsibility; continuous improvement in work; adaptability and flexibility; human relationship in work; punctuality; time management; initiation and autonomy; innovation and creativity; teamwork; relation with public; resources management. In addition, the target Macau, China sets is to meet timelines set by the internal guidelines to ensure there is no undue delay caused by its competent authority.

135. The Action 14 final report (OECD, 2015) includes examples of performance indicators that are considered appropriate. These indicators are shown below in bullet form:

- number of MAP cases resolved
- consistency (i.e. a treaty should be applied in a principled and consistent manner to MAP cases involving the same facts and similarly-situated taxpayers)

- time taken to resolve a MAP case (recognising that the time taken to resolve a MAP case may vary according to its complexity and that matters not under the control of a competent authority may have a significant impact on the time needed to resolve a case).

136. Macau, China reported that it does not use any performance indicators for staff in charge of MAP that are related to the outcome of MAP discussions in terms of the amount of sustained audit adjustments or maintained tax revenue. In other words, staff in charge of MAP would not be evaluated on the basis of the material outcome of MAP discussions.

Recent developments

137. There are no recent developments with respect to element C.5.

Practical application

138. No peer input was provided.

Anticipated modifications

139. Macau, China indicated that it does not anticipate any modifications in relation to element C.5.

Conclusion

	Areas for improvement	Recommendations
[C.5]	-	-

[C.6] Provide transparency with respect to the position on MAP arbitration

> Jurisdictions should provide transparency with respect to their positions on MAP arbitration.

140. The inclusion of an arbitration provision in tax treaties may help ensure that MAP cases are resolved within a certain timeframe, which provides certainty to both taxpayers and competent authorities. In order to have full clarity on whether arbitration as a final stage in the MAP process can and will be available in jurisdictions it is important that jurisdictions are transparent on their position on MAP arbitration.

Position on MAP arbitration

141. Macau, China reported that it has no domestic law limitations for including MAP arbitration in its tax treaties but that MAP arbitration is not currently available for the resolution of tax treaty related disputes in any of its tax treaties. This is clarified in Macau, China's MAP profile.

Recent developments

142. There are no recent developments with respect to element C.6.

Practical application

143. Macau, China has not incorporated an arbitration clause in any of its six tax treaties as a final stage to the MAP.

Anticipated modifications

144. Macau, China indicated that it does not anticipate any modifications in relation to element C.6.

Conclusion

	Areas for improvement	Recommendations
[C.6]	-	-

References

OECD (2015), "Making Dispute Resolution Mechanisms More Effective, Action 14 – 2015 Final Report", in *OECD/G20 Base Erosion and Profit Shifting Project*, OECD Publishing, Paris, https://dx.doi.org/10.1787/9789264241633-en.

OECD (2017), *Model Tax Convention on Income and on Capital 2017 (Full Version)*, OECD Publishing, Paris, https://dx.doi.org/10.1787/g2g972ee-en.

Part D

Implementation of MAP agreements

[D.1] Implement all MAP agreements

> Jurisdictions should implement any agreement reached in MAP discussions, including by making appropriate adjustments to the tax assessed in transfer pricing cases.

145. In order to provide full certainty to taxpayers and the jurisdictions, it is essential that all MAP agreements are implemented by the competent authorities concerned.

Legal framework to implement MAP agreements

146. Macau, China reported that the Complementary Tax Regulation (1978) stipulates that the time limit for tax assessment is five years, which applies to upward adjustments, while there is no time limit for downward adjustment. Macau, China also reported that internal law limitations will not jeopardise or preclude the application and implementation of a MAP outcome, and any agreement reached under a MAP shall be implemented notwithstanding any time limits in the internal laws of Macau, China in accordance with the applicable treaty. As discussed under element D.3, all of Macau, China's treaties contain a provision equivalent to Article 25(2) second sentence, stating that all MAP agreements shall be implemented notwithstanding any domestic time limits, following which the domestic statute of limitation would not be applicable.

147. Section 6 of Macau, China's MAP guidance describes the procedure that would apply after a MAP agreement is reached. This section notes that Macau, China's competent authority will notify the taxpayer the terms and conditions of the agreement. If the taxpayer confirms its acceptance of the agreement within 30 days, where such acceptance obliges the taxpayer to withdraw any pending cases in the judicial or administrative instances, Macau, China reported that its tax authority will confirm the agreement in writing with the competent authority of the other party. On the other hand, Macau, China's MAP guidance further describes that if the taxpayer does not accept the terms and conditions of such agreement within 30 days, the competent authority send the competent authority of the other party a proposal to close the MAP case without agreement.

Recent developments

148. There are no recent developments with respect to element D.1.

Practical application

Period 1 January 2016-31 August 2019 (stage 1)

149. Macau, China reported that no MAP agreements requiring implementation were reached in the period 1 January 2016-31 August 2019.

150. No peer input was provided.

Period 1 September 2019-30 April 2021 (stage 2)

151. Macau, China reported that no MAP agreements requiring implementation were reached since 1 September 2019 as well.

152. No peer input was provided.

Anticipated modifications

153. Macau, China indicated that it does not anticipate any modifications in relation to element D.1.

Conclusion

	Areas for improvement	Recommendations
[D.1]	-	-

[D.2] Implement all MAP agreements on a timely basis

> Agreements reached by competent authorities through the MAP process should be implemented on a timely basis.

154. Delay of implementation of MAP agreements may lead to adverse financial consequences for both taxpayers and competent authorities. To avoid this and to increase certainty for all parties involved, it is important that the implementation of any MAP agreement is not obstructed by procedural and/or statutory delays in the jurisdictions concerned.

Theoretical timeframe for implementing mutual agreements

155. Macau, China reported that there is no theoretical timeframe for implementing mutual agreements, but Macau, China expects that a MAP will be implemented in less than 30 days. In addition, Macau, China's MAP guidance describes that its competent authority will promote the swift implementation of MAP agreements.

Recent developments

156. There are no recent developments with respect to element D.2.

Practical application

Period 1 January 2016-31 August 2019 (stage 1)

157. Macau, China reported that no MAP agreements requiring implementation were reached in the period 1 January 2016-31 August 2019.

158. No peer input was provided.

Period 1 September 2019-30 April 2021 (stage 2)

159. Macau, China reported that no MAP agreements requiring implementation were reached since 1 September 2019 as well.

160. No peer input was provided.

Anticipated modifications

161. Macau, China indicated that it does not anticipate any modifications in relation to element D.2.

Conclusion

	Areas for improvement	Recommendations
[D.2]	-	-

[D.3] Include Article 25(2), second sentence, of the OECD Model Tax Convention in tax treaties or alternative provisions in Article 9(1) and Article 7(2)

> Jurisdictions should either (i) provide in their tax treaties that any mutual agreement reached through MAP shall be implemented notwithstanding any time limits in their domestic law, or (ii) be willing to accept alternative treaty provisions that limit the time during which a Contracting Party may make an adjustment pursuant to Article 9(1) or Article 7(2), in order to avoid late adjustments with respect to which MAP relief will not be available.

162. In order to provide full certainty to taxpayers it is essential that implementation of MAP agreements is not obstructed by any time limits in the domestic law of the jurisdictions concerned. Such certainty can be provided by either including the equivalent of Article 25(2), second sentence, of the OECD Model Tax Convention (OECD, 2017) in tax treaties, or alternatively, setting a time limit in Article 9(1) and Article 7(2) for making adjustments to avoid that late adjustments obstruct granting of MAP relief.

Legal framework and current situation of Macau, China's tax treaties

163. All of Macau, China's six tax treaties contain a provision equivalent to Article 25(2), second sentence, of the OECD Model Tax Convention (OECD, 2017) that any mutual agreement reached through MAP shall be implemented notwithstanding any time limits in their domestic law.

Recent developments

Bilateral modifications

164. Macau, China signed a new tax treaty with one treaty partner which is a newly negotiated treaty with a treaty partner with which there was no treaty yet in place. This treaty has not entered into force as yet. This treaty includes a provision that is equivalent to Article 25(2), second sentence, of the OECD Model Tax Convention (OECD, 2017). The effect of this newly signed treaty has been reflected in the analysis above where it has relevance.

Peer input

165. No peer input was provided.

Anticipated modifications

Bilateral modifications

166. Macau, China reported it will seek to include Article 25(2), second sentence, of the OECD Model Tax Convention (OECD, 2017) or both alternatives in all of its future tax treaties.

Conclusion

	Areas for improvement	Recommendations
[D.3]	-	-

Reference

OECD (2017), *Model Tax Convention on Income and on Capital 2017 (Full Version)*, OECD Publishing, Paris, https://dx.doi.org/10.1787/g2g972ee-en.

Summary

	Areas for improvement	Recommendations
Part A: Preventing disputes		
[A.1]	-	-
[A.2]	-	-
Part B: Availability and access to MAP		
[B.1]	One out of six tax treaties does not contain a provision that is equivalent to Article 25(1), first sentence, of the OECD Model Tax Convention (OECD, 2015a), either as it read prior to the adoption of the Action 14 final report or as amended by that report (OECD, 2015b). With respect to this treaty, negotiations are on-going.	For the treaty that does not contain the equivalent of Article 25(1) of the OECD Model Tax Convention (OECD, 2015a), as it read prior to the adoption of the Action 14 final report (OECD, 2015b), Macau, China should continue negotiations with the treaty partner with a view to including the required provision. This concerns a provision that is equivalent to Article 25(1), first sentence of the OECD Model Tax Convention (OECD, 2015a) either: a. as amended in the Action 14 final report (OECD, 2015b); or b. as it read prior to the adoption of the Action 14 final report (OECD, 2015b), thereby including the full sentence of such provision.
[B.2]	-	-
[B.3]	-	-
[B.4]	-	-
[B.5]	-	-
[B.6]	-	-
[B.7]	One out of six tax treaties does not contain a provision that is equivalent to Article 25(3), second sentence, of the OECD Model Tax Convention (OECD, 2017). With respect to this treaty, negotiations are envisaged.	For the treaty that does not contain the equivalent of Article 25(3), second sentence, of the OECD Model Tax Convention (OECD, 2017), Macau, China should continue (the initiation of) negotiations with the treaty partner with a view to including the required provision.
[B.8]	-	-
[B.9]	-	-
[B.10]	-	-
Part C: Resolution of MAP cases		
[C.1]	-	-
[C.2]	-	-
[C.3]	-	-
[C.4]	-	-
[C.5]	-	-

	Areas for improvement	Recommendations
[C.6]	-	-
Part D: Implementation of MAP agreements		
[D.1]	-	-
[D.2]	-	-
[D.3]	-	-

Annex A

Tax treaty network of Macau, China

Treaty partner	DTC in force? Y = yes N = signed pending ratification	If N, date of signing	Article 25(1) of the OECD Model Tax Convention ("MTC")			Article 9(2) of the OECD MTC	Anti-abuse	Article 25(2) of the OECD MTC		Article 25(3) of the OECD MTC		Arbitration
			B.1 Column 3 Inclusion Art. 25(1) first sentence? If yes, submission to either competent authority? (new Art. 25(1), first sentence) E = yes, either CAs O = yes, only one CA N = No	B.1 Column 4 Inclusion Art. 25(1) second sentence? (Note 1) Y = yes i = no, no such provision ii = no, different period iii = no, starting point for computing the 3 year period is different iv = no, other reasons	If no, please state reasons / if ii, specify period	B.3 Column 5 Inclusion Art. 9(2) (Note 2) If no, will your CA provide access to MAP in TP cases? Y = yes i = no, but access will be given to TP cases ii = no and access will not be given to TP cases	B.4 Column 6 Inclusion provision that MAP Article will not be available in cases where your jurisdiction is of the assessment that there is an abuse of the DTC or of the domestic tax law? If no, will your CA accept a taxpayer's request for MAP in relation to such cases? Y = yes i = no and such cases will be accepted for MAP ii = no but such cases will not be accepted for MAP	C.1 Column 7 Inclusion Art. 25(2) first sentence? (Note 3)	D.3 Column 8 Inclusion Art. 25(2) second sentence? (Note 4) If no, alternative provision in Art. 7 & 9 OECD MTC? (Note 4) Y = yes i = no, but have Art. 7 equivalent ii = no, but have Art. 9 equivalent iii = no, but have both Art. 7 & 9 equivalent N = no and no equivalent of Art. 7 and 9	A.1 Column 9 Inclusion Art. 25(3) first sentence? (Note 5) Y = yes N = no	B.7 Column 10 Inclusion Art. 25(3) second sentence? (Note 6) Y = yes N = no	C.6 Column 11 Inclusion arbitration provision? Y = yes N = no
Belgium	N	6/19/2006	O	Y	N/A	Y	i	Y	Y	Y	N	N
Cambodia	N	4/23/2021	E	Y	N/A	Y	i	Y	Y	Y	Y	N
Cape Verde	Y	N/A	O	Y	N/A	Y	i	Y	Y	Y	Y	N
Mozambique	Y	N/A	N	Y	N/A	Y	i	Y	Y	Y	Y	N
Portugal	Y	N/A	O	Y	N/A	Y	i	Y	Y	Y	Y	N
Viet Nam	Y	N/A	O	Y	N/A	Y	i	Y	Y	Y	Y	N

Legend	
E*	The provision contained in this treaty was already in line with the requirements under this element of the Action 14 Minimum Standard, but has been modified by the Multilateral Instrument to allow the filing of a MAP request in either contracting state.
E**	The provision contained in this treaty was not in line with the requirements under this element of the Action 14 Minimum Standard, but the treaty has been modified by the Multilateral Instrument and is now in line with this standard.
O*	The provision contained in this treaty is already in line with the requirements under this element of the Action 14 Minimum Standard, but will be modified by the Multilateral Instrument upon entry into force for this specific treaty and will then allow the filing of a MAP request in either contracting state.
Y*	The provision contained in this treaty was not in line with the requirements under this element of the Action 14 Minimum Standard, but the treaty has been modified by the Multilateral Instrument and is now in line with this element of the Action 14 Minimum Standard.
Y**	The provision contained in this treaty already included an arbitration provision, which has been replaced by part VI of the Multilateral Instrument containing a mandatory and binding arbitration procedure.
Y***	The provision contained in this treaty did not include an arbitration provision, but part VI of the Multilateral Instrument applies, following which a mandatory and binding arbitration procedure is included in this treaty
i*/ii*/iv*/N*	The provision contained in this treaty is not in line with the requirements under this element of the Action 14 Minimum Standard, but the treaty will be modified by the Multilateral Instrument upon entry into force for this specific treaty and will then be in line with this element of the Action 14 Minimum Standard.
i**/iv**/N**	The provision contained in this treaty is not in line with the requirements under this element of the Action 14 Minimum Standard, but the treaty will be superseded by the Multilateral Instrument upon entry into force for this specific treaty only to the extent that existing treaty provisions are incompatible with the relevant provision of the Multilateral Instrument.
i***	The provision contained in this treaty is not in line with the requirements under this element of the Action 14 Minimum Standard, but the treaty will be superseded by the Multilateral Instrument only to the extent that existing treaty provisions are incompatible with the relevant provision of the Multilateral Instrument.

Annex B

MAP Statistics Reporting for the 2016, 2017, 2018, 2019 and 2020 Reporting Periods (1 January 2016 to 31 December 2020) for pre-2016 cases

2016 MAP Statistics

Category of cases	No. of pre-2016 cases in MAP inventory on 1 January 2016	Number of pre-2016 cases closed during the reporting period by outcome										No. of pre-2017 cases remaining in on MAP inventory on 31 December 2016	Average time taken (in months) for closing pre-2016 cases during the reporting period
		Denied MAP access	Objection is not justified	Withdrawn by taxpayer	Unilateral relief granted	Resolved via domestic remedy	Agreement fully eliminating double taxation/ fully resolving taxation not in accordance with tax treaty	Agreement partially eliminating double taxation/partially resolving taxation not in accordance with tax treaty	Agreement that there is no taxation not in accordance with tax treaty	No agreement, including agreement to disagree	Any other outcome		
Column 1	Column 2	Column 3	Column 4	Column 5	Column 6	Column 7	Column 8	Column 9	Column 10	Column 11	Column 12	Column 13	Column 14
Attribution/ Allocation	0	0	0	0	0	0	0	0	0	0	0	0	N/A
Others	0	0	0	0	0	0	0	0	0	0	0	0	N/A
Total	0	0	0	0	0	0	0	0	0	0	0	0	N/A

2017 MAP Statistics

Category of cases	No. of pre-2016 cases in MAP inventory on 1 January 2017	Number of pre-2016 cases closed during the reporting period by outcome										No. of pre-2017 cases remaining in on MAP inventory on 31 December 2017	Average time taken (in months) for closing pre-2016 cases during the reporting period
		Denied MAP access	Objection is not justified	Withdrawn by taxpayer	Unilateral relief granted	Resolved via domestic remedy	Agreement fully eliminating double taxation/ fully resolving taxation not in accordance with tax treaty	Agreement partially eliminating double taxation/partially resolving taxation not in accordance with tax treaty	Agreement that there is no taxation not in accordance with tax treaty	No agreement, including agreement to disagree	Any other outcome		
Column 1	Column 2	Column 3	Column 4	Column 5	Column 6	Column 7	Column 8	Column 9	Column 10	Column 11	Column 12	Column 13	Column 14
Attribution/ Allocation	0	0	0	0	0	0	0	0	0	0	0	0	N/A
Others	0	0	0	0	0	0	0	0	0	0	0	0	N/A
Total	0	0	0	0	0	0	0	0	0	0	0	0	N/A

2018 MAP Statistics

Category of cases	No. of pre-2016 cases in MAP inventory on 1 January 2018	Denied MAP access	Objection is not justified	Withdrawn by taxpayer	Unilateral relief granted	Resolved via domestic remedy	Agreement fully eliminating double taxation/ fully resolving taxation not in accordance with tax treaty	Agreement partially eliminating double taxation/partially resolving taxation not in accordance with tax treaty	Agreement that there is no taxation not in accordance with tax treaty	No agreement, including agreement to disagree	Any other outcome	No. of pre-2017 cases remaining in on MAP inventory on 31 December 2018	Average time taken (in months) for closing pre-2016 cases during the reporting period
Column 1	Column 2	Column 3	Column 4	Column 5	Column 6	Column 7	Column 8	Column 9	Column 10	Column 11	Column 12	Column 13	Column 14
Attribution/Allocation	0	0	0	0	0	0	0	0	0	0	0	0	N/A
Others	0	0	0	0	0	0	0	0	0	0	0	0	N/A
Total	0	0	0	0	0	0	0	0	0	0	0	0	N/A

2019 MAP Statistics

Category of cases	No. of pre-2016 cases in MAP inventory on 1 January 2019	Denied MAP access	Objection is not justified	Withdrawn by taxpayer	Unilateral relief granted	Resolved via domestic remedy	Agreement fully eliminating double taxation/ fully resolving taxation not in accordance with tax treaty	Agreement partially eliminating double taxation/partially resolving taxation not in accordance with tax treaty	Agreement that there is no taxation not in accordance with tax treaty	No agreement, including agreement to disagree	Any other outcome	No. of pre-2017 cases remaining in on MAP inventory on 31 December 2019	Average time taken (in months) for closing pre-2016 cases during the reporting period
Column 1	Column 2	Column 3	Column 4	Column 5	Column 6	Column 7	Column 8	Column 9	Column 10	Column 11	Column 12	Column 13	Column 14
Attribution/Allocation	0	0	0	0	0	0	0	0	0	0	0	0	N/A
Others	0	0	0	0	0	0	0	0	0	0	0	0	N/A
Total	0	0	0	0	0	0	0	0	0	0	0	0	N/A

2020 MAP Statistics

Category of cases	No. of pre-2016 cases in MAP inventory on 1 January 2020	Number of pre-2016 cases closed during the reporting period by outcome									No. of pre-2017 cases remaining in on MAP inventory on 31 December 2020	Average time taken (in months) for closing pre-2016 cases during the reporting period
		Denied MAP access	Objection is not justified	Withdrawn by taxpayer	Unilateral relief granted	Resolved via domestic remedy	Agreement fully eliminating double taxation/ fully resolving taxation not in accordance with tax treaty	Agreement partially eliminating double taxation/partially resolving taxation not in accordance with tax treaty	Agreement that there is no taxation not in accordance with tax treaty	No agreement, including agreement to disagree	Any other outcome		
	Column 2	Column 3	Column 4	Column 5	Column 6	Column 7	Column 8	Column 9	Column 10	Column 11	Column 12	Column 13	Column 14
Column 1													
Attribution/ Allocation	0	0	0	0	0	0	0	0	0	0	0	0	N/A
Others	0	0	0	0	0	0	0	0	0	0	0	0	N/A
Total	0	0	0	0	0	0	0	0	0	0	0	0	N/A

Annex C

MAP Statistics Reporting for the 2016, 2017, 2018, 2019 and 2020 Reporting Periods
(1 January 2016 to 31 December 2020) for post-2015 cases

2016 MAP Statistics

Category of cases	No. of post-2015 cases in MAP inventory on 1 January 2016	No. of post-2015 cases started during the reporting period	Number of post-2015 cases closed during the reporting period by outcome									No. of post-2015 cases remaining in MAP inventory on 31 December 2016	Average time taken (in months) for closing post-2015 cases during the reporting period
			Denied MAP access	Objection is not justified	Withdrawn by taxpayer	Unilateral relief granted	Resolved via domestic remedy	Agreement fully eliminating double taxation/ fully resolving taxation not in accordance with tax treaty	Agreement partially eliminating double taxation/partially resolving taxation not in accordance with tax treaty	Agreement that there is no taxation not in accordance with tax treaty	No agreement, including agreement to disagree	Any other outcome		
Column 1	Column 2	Column 3	Column 4	Column 5	Column 6	Column 7	Column 8	Column 9	Column 10	Column 11	Column 12	Column 13	Column 14	Column 15
Attribution/ Allocation	0	0	0	0	0	0	0	0	0	0	0	0	0	N/A
Others	0	0	0	0	0	0	0	0	0	0	0	0	0	N/A
Total	0	0	0	0	0	0	0	0	0	0	0	0	0	N/A

2017 MAP Statistics

Category of cases	No. of post-2015 cases in MAP inventory on 1 January 2017	No. of post-2015 cases started during the reporting period	Number of post-2015 cases closed during the reporting period by outcome									No. of post-2015 cases remaining in MAP inventory on 31 December 2017	Average time taken (in months) for closing post-2015 cases during the reporting period
			Denied MAP access	Objection is not justified	Withdrawn by taxpayer	Unilateral relief granted	Resolved via domestic remedy	Agreement fully eliminating double taxation/ fully resolving taxation not in accordance with tax treaty	Agreement partially eliminating double taxation/partially resolving taxation not in accordance with tax treaty	Agreement that there is no taxation not in accordance with tax treaty	No agreement, including agreement to disagree	Any other outcome		
Column 1	Column 2	Column 3	Column 4	Column 5	Column 6	Column 7	Column 8	Column 9	Column 10	Column 11	Column 12	Column 13	Column 14	Column 15
Attribution/ Allocation	0	0	0	0	0	0	0	0	0	0	0	0	0	N/A
Others	0	0	0	0	0	0	0	0	0	0	0	0	0	N/A
Total	0	0	0	0	0	0	0	0	0	0	0	0	0	N/A

2018 MAP Statistics

Category of cases	No. of post-2015 cases in MAP inventory on 1 January 2018	No. of post-2015 cases started during the reporting period	Number of post-2015 cases closed during the reporting period by outcome										No. of post-2015 cases remaining in on MAP inventory on 31 December 2018	Average time taken (in months) for closing post-2015 cases during the reporting period
			Denied MAP access	Objection is not justified	Withdrawn by taxpayer	Unilateral relief granted	Resolved via domestic remedy	Agreement fully eliminating double taxation/ fully resolving taxation not in accordance with tax treaty	Agreement partially eliminating double taxation/partially resolving taxation not in accordance with tax treaty	Agreement that there is no taxation not in accordance with tax treaty	No agreement, including agreement to disagree	Any other outcome		
Column 1	Column 2	Column 3	Column 4	Column 5	Column 6	Column 7	Column 8	Column 9	Column 10	Column 11	Column 12	Column 13	Column 14	Column 15
Attribution/Allocation	0	0	0	0	0	0	0	0	0	0	0	0	0	N/A
Others	0	0	0	0	0	0	0	0	0	0	0	0	0	N/A
Total	0	0	0	0	0	0	0	0	0	0	0	0	0	N/A

2019 MAP Statistics

Category of cases	No. of post-2015 cases in MAP inventory on 1 January 2019	No. of post-2015 cases started during the reporting period	Number of post-2015 cases closed during the reporting period by outcome										No. of post-2015 cases remaining in on MAP inventory on 31 December 2019	Average time taken (in months) for closing post-2015 cases during the reporting period
			Denied MAP access	Objection is not justified	Withdrawn by taxpayer	Unilateral relief granted	Resolved via domestic remedy	Agreement fully eliminating double taxation/ fully resolving taxation not in accordance with tax treaty	Agreement partially eliminating double taxation/partially resolving taxation not in accordance with tax treaty	Agreement that there is no taxation not in accordance with tax treaty	No agreement, including agreement to disagree	Any other outcome		
Column 1	Column 2	Column 3	Column 4	Column 5	Column 6	Column 7	Column 8	Column 9	Column 10	Column 11	Column 12	Column 13	Column 14	Column 15
Attribution/Allocation	0	0	0	0	0	0	0	0	0	0	0	0	0	N/A
Others	0	0	0	0	0	0	0	0	0	0	0	0	0	N/A
Total	0	0	0	0	0	0	0	0	0	0	0	0	0	N/A

2020 MAP Statistics

Number of post-2015 cases closed during the reporting period by outcome

Category of cases	No. of post-2015 cases in MAP inventory on 1 January 2020	No. of post-2015 cases started during the reporting period	Denied MAP access	Objection is not justified	Withdrawn by taxpayer	Unilateral relief granted	Resolved via domestic remedy	Agreement fully eliminating double taxation/ fully resolving taxation not in accordance with tax treaty	Agreement partially eliminating double taxation/partially resolving taxation not in accordance with tax treaty	Agreement that there is no taxation not in accordance with tax treaty	No agreement, including agreement to disagree	Any other outcome	No. of post-2015 cases remaining in on MAP inventory on 31 December 2020	Average time taken (in months) for closing post-2015 cases during the reporting period
	Column 2	Column 3	Column 4	Column 5	Column 6	Column 7	Column 8	Column 9	Column 10	Column 11	Column 12	Column 13	Column 14	Column 15
Attribution/ Allocation	0	0	0	0	0	0	0	0	0	0	0	0	0	N/A
Others	0	0	0	0	0	0	0	0	0	0	0	0	0	N/A
Total	0	0	0	0	0	0	0	0	0	0	0	0	0	N/A

Glossary

Action 14 Minimum Standard	The minimum standard as agreed upon in the final report on Action 14: Making Dispute Resolution Mechanisms More Effective
MAP Guidance	Mutual Agreement Procedure Guidelines
MAP Statistics Reporting Framework	Rules for reporting of MAP statistics as agreed by the FTA MAP Forum
OECD Model Tax Convention (OECD, 2017)	OECD Model Tax Convention on Income and on Capital as it read on 21 November 2017
OECD Transfer Pricing Guidelines	OECD Transfer Pricing Guidelines for Multinational Enterprises and Tax Administrations
Pre-2016 cases	MAP cases in a competent authority's inventory that are pending resolution on 31 December 2015
Post-2015 cases	MAP cases that are received by a competent authority from the taxpayer on or after 1 January 2016
Statistics Reporting Period	Period for reporting MAP statistics that started on 1 January 2016 and ended on 31 December 2020
Terms of Reference	Terms of reference to monitor and review the implementing of the BEPS Action 14 Minimum Standard to make dispute resolution mechanisms more effective

www.ingramcontent.com/pod-product-compliance
Lightning Source LLC
Chambersburg PA
CBHW062159220526
45470CB00009B/2870